Crafting the Seamless User Experience

A Guide to UX/UI Design Principles

Benjamin Evans

DEDICATION

Dedicated to those who dream, create, and imagine; to the seekers of wisdom, and the believers in the power of words. May this book be a companion on your journey, igniting your imagination, stirring your soul, and inspiring your own unique tale in the vast narrative of life.

CONTENTS

ACKNOWLEDGMENTS

I would like to express my sincere gratitude to all those who have contributed to the realization of this book. To my family and friends, whose unwavering support and encouragement have been a constant source of inspiration. To my mentors and advisors, for their guidance, wisdom, and belief in my abilities. To the countless individuals whose insights, feedback, and contributions have enriched these pages. And to the readers, whose curiosity and passion for knowledge drive the pursuit of storytelling. Thank you for being a part of this journey.

CHAPTER 1

Introduction to UX/UI Design

Welcome to the exciting world of UX/UI design! In this chapter, we'll embark on a journey to understand what UX and UI design are, why they're so important, and how they work together to create seamless user experiences.

1.1 What is UX Design?

UX, or User Experience design, focuses on the **entire journey** a user takes when interacting with a product, service, or digital platform. Imagine walking into a physical store. A good UX design considers everything from how easily you find the entrance to the store, the layout that guides you to desired products, the intuitiveness of the checkout process, and even the helpfulness of the staff. In the digital world, UX design encompasses aspects like:

- **User research:** Understanding your target

audience's needs, goals, and pain points.

- **Information architecture:** Structuring content in a logical and easy-to-find way.
- **Interaction design:** Crafting user flows that are intuitive and efficient for completing tasks.
- **Usability:** Ensuring the interface is clear, easy to navigate, and minimizes user frustration.

A successful UX design anticipates user needs and creates a journey that is not only functional but also enjoyable and engaging.

1.2 What is UI Design?

UI, or User Interface design, focuses on the **visual elements** that a user interacts with. Continuing with our store analogy, UI design would be the look and feel of the store itself. This includes:

- **Layout:** The arrangement of elements on the screen or page.
- **Visual hierarchy:** Guiding the user's eye to the most important information.
- **Typography:** Selecting fonts that are easy to read

and complement the overall design style.

- **Color scheme:** Using color strategically to create a visually appealing and functional interface.
- **Buttons, icons, and other interactive elements:** Ensuring they are clear, consistent, and provide good user feedback.

Effective UI design creates a visually appealing and intuitive interface that users can easily understand and interact with.

1.3 Why is UX/UI Design Important?

In today's digital age, users have high expectations for the products and services they interact with. A well-designed UX/UI experience offers several benefits:

- **Increased User Satisfaction:** When users can easily find what they need and complete tasks with minimal frustration, they are more likely to be satisfied with the product or service.
- **Improved Brand Reputation:** A seamless user experience reflects positively on your brand, fostering trust and loyalty.

- **Enhanced User Engagement:** Intuitive design keeps users engaged with your product, encouraging them to explore further and return for more.

- **Boosted Business Growth:** A positive user experience translates to increased sales, conversions, and customer retention.

By prioritizing UX/UI design, you're not just creating interfaces; you're crafting experiences that resonate with users and drive business success.

UX and UI design are two sides of the same coin. They work together to create a holistic and user-centered approach to digital product development. In the following chapters, we'll delve deeper into each of these areas and explore the principles that guide successful UX/UI design.

CHAPTER 2

User-Centered Design

The foundation of exceptional UX/UI design lies in understanding the people you're designing for. This chapter dives into the concept of user-centered design, exploring techniques to understand your users and build robust user personas.

2.1 Understanding Your Users

Imagine designing a mobile app without knowing who will use it. Odds are, it won't be very successful. User-centered design flips this approach on its head. It prioritizes understanding your users' needs, goals, and behaviors to create an experience that truly resonates with them. Here's why it matters:

- **Reduced Risk of Failure:** By understanding user needs upfront, you avoid pouring resources into features or interfaces that nobody wants.

- **Increased User Adoption:** When your design addresses user pain points and facilitates their goals, they're more likely to embrace it.

- **Enhanced User Satisfaction:** User-centered design fosters a sense of empathy and understanding, leading to a more satisfying experience.

So, how do we truly understand our users? Here are some key strategies:

- **Empathy:** Put yourself in your users' shoes. Consider their daily routines, challenges, and motivations.

2.2 User Research Techniques

User research is the cornerstone of understanding your user base. Here are some valuable techniques to gather valuable insights:

- **User Interviews:** One-on-one conversations with target users to delve into their experiences, needs, and frustrations.

- **Surveys and Questionnaires:** Gather broader user

data through online or paper surveys and questionnaires.

- **Usability Testing:** Observe users interacting with prototypes or existing interfaces to identify usability issues.
- **Card Sorting:** Have users categorize information to understand how they organize content intuitively.
- **Competitive Analysis:** Analyze how your competitors approach UX/UI design for similar products.

It's important to note: User research is an iterative process. The insights you gather will inform your design decisions, and as you prototype and test your designs, you'll gain further user feedback that can refine your understanding.

2.3 Building User Personas

Once you've gathered user research data, it's time to synthesize it into user personas. These are fictional characters that represent your target audience segments. A well-crafted persona goes beyond demographics. It includes:

- **Goals and Needs:** What does this user want to achieve? What pain points do they experience?
- **Behaviors and Attitudes:** How does this user typically interact with similar products? What are their expectations?
- **Skills and Technical Knowledge:** What level of technical expertise does this user possess?
- **Background and Context:** Consider the user's social context, values, and motivations.

By creating user personas, you gain a deeper understanding of your target audience. These personas become a reference point throughout the design process, ensuring your decisions remain user-centered.

User research and building user personas are ongoing processes. As your product evolves or market trends shift, revisiting your user understanding is crucial for maintaining a user-centered approach.

In the next chapter, we'll explore the principles of designing for usability, ensuring your user interface is not just beautiful but also functional and intuitive.

CHAPTER 3

DESIGNING FOR USABILITY

Now that you understand your users, it's time to translate that knowledge into a usable interface. This chapter explores the core principles of usability and dives into the fundamental considerations for both UI design and UX design.

3.1 The Principles of Usability

Usability refers to the ease with which users can interact with and achieve their goals within a product or interface. Here are some key principles to guide your design for usability:

- **Learnability:** How easily can users understand and learn how to use the interface? Strive for intuitive design that minimizes the learning curve.
- **Efficiency:** Can users complete tasks quickly and with minimal effort? Optimize workflows for

efficiency and minimize unnecessary steps.

- **Memorability:** Can users remember how to use the interface after some time away? Maintain consistency in design patterns and user flows.

- **Error Prevention:** Can errors be prevented or easily recovered from? Implement clear error messages and provide guidance for users to get back on track.

- **Satisfaction:** Do users find the experience enjoyable and fulfilling? Prioritize user satisfaction by creating a clear, consistent, and aesthetically pleasing interface.

By adhering to these principles, you create a user interface that is not only functional but also enjoyable and promotes user satisfaction.

3.2 User Interface (UI) Design Fundamentals

The visual elements of your interface play a crucial role in usability. Here are some fundamental UI design considerations:

- **Visual Hierarchy:** Guide the user's eye to the most important information through size, color, and positioning.

- **Clarity and Consistency:** Use clear language, consistent typography, and predictable layouts throughout the interface.

- **Accessibility:** Ensure your interface is usable by everyone, including users with disabilities. Follow accessibility guidelines like WCAG (Web Content Accessibility Guidelines).

- **White Space:** Strategic use of white space improves readability and prevents the interface from feeling cluttered.

- **Feedback and Affordance:** Provide clear feedback to users on their actions, and make interactive elements visually represent their functionality (e.g., a button should look like something you can press).

These UI design fundamentals contribute significantly to creating an intuitive and user-friendly interface.

3.3 User Interaction (UX) Design Considerations

Beyond the visuals, user interaction design focuses on how users navigate and complete tasks within your interface.

Here are some key UX design considerations:

- **User Flows:** Map out the various user journeys and interactions within your product. Ensure these flows are logical and efficient.
- **Navigation Systems:** Design clear and intuitive navigation menus and structures that allow users to find what they need easily.
- **Search Functionality:** If your interface involves a large amount of content, implement a robust and user-friendly search function.
- **Form Design:** Create clear and concise forms that minimize user effort when entering information.
- **Error Handling and Recovery:** Design user-friendly error messages that guide users towards resolving issues.

By focusing on these UX design considerations, you ensure a smooth and efficient user experience that facilitates users in achieving their goals.

Usability is an ongoing process. Always test your designs with real users and iterate based on their feedback. The more usable your interface is, the higher the user satisfaction and the greater the success of your product.

CHAPTER 4

INFORMATION ARCHITECTURE AND NAVIGATION

Imagine walking into a library without a Dewey Decimal System or any organization. Finding the book you need would be a nightmare! Just like a library, digital products also require a well-defined structure for users to navigate content effectively. This chapter explores the concepts of information architecture (IA) and navigation, the cornerstones of a user-friendly experience.

4.1 Organizing Content for Easy Access

Information architecture (IA) refers to the art and science of organizing content within a digital product. It's like the blueprint for your website or app, determining how content is categorized, labeled, and connected. Effective IA ensures:

- **Findability:** Users can easily locate the information they're looking for.

- **Usability:** Users can navigate the interface with minimal effort.
- **Discoverability:** Users can stumble upon unexpected but relevant content, enhancing their experience.

Here are some key strategies for organizing content:

- **Content Inventory:** Create a comprehensive list of all the content within your product.
- **User Needs Analysis:** Understand what users are looking for and how they categorize information.
- **Card Sorting:** Engage users in sorting exercises to see how they naturally group related content.
- **Content Labeling:** Use clear and concise language to label content categories and elements.

By prioritizing organization and clear labeling, you create an information architecture that empowers users to find what they need intuitively.

4.2 Navigation Systems and Patterns

Navigation systems are the tools users employ to move

around your interface and access different sections of content. Common navigation systems include:

- **Global Navigation (Top Menu):** Provides persistent links to major sections of the website or app, typically located at the top of the page.
- **Local Navigation (Breadcrumbs):** Shows the user's current location within the information hierarchy, often displayed as a breadcrumb trail.
- **Search Functionality:** Allows users to find specific information by keyword or phrase.
- **Facets and Filters:** Enables users to refine search results based on specific criteria.

Effective navigation leverages established patterns that users are familiar with. This consistency minimizes the learning curve and promotes intuitive exploration of your product.

4.3 Creating a Clear Information Hierarchy

Information hierarchy refers to the organization of content based on its importance and user needs. Imagine a pyramid, with the most critical information at the top and more specific details branching out below. Here's how to create a clear information hierarchy:

- **Identify Core User Tasks:** Understand the primary goals users want to accomplish within your product.
- **Prioritize Content:** Rank content based on its relevance to user tasks and overall importance.
- **Group Related Content:** Organize content into logical categories and subcategories.
- **Visual Hierarchy:** Use visual cues like size, color, and spacing to guide users towards the most important information.

By creating a clear information hierarchy, you ensure that users can easily find and understand the content that is most relevant to them.

Information architecture and navigation are intertwined. A well-defined IA lays the foundation for intuitive navigation systems, ultimately leading to a seamless user experience. In the next chapter, we'll explore the world of visual design and branding, delving into how aesthetics can enhance usability and user engagement.

CHAPTER 5

VISUAL DESIGN AND BRANDING

The visual elements of your interface play a crucial role not only in usability but also in user perception and brand recognition. This chapter dives into the world of visual design and branding, exploring how aesthetics can elevate user experience and create a lasting impression.

5.1 Visual Hierarchy and Design Principles

Visual hierarchy refers to the arrangement of elements on your interface to guide the user's eye towards the most important information. Just like a well-written paragraph, your interface should have a clear visual flow that directs user attention. Here are some key design principles to achieve this:

- **Balance:** Arrange elements in a way that feels visually pleasing and stable. Asymmetry can also be used strategically to create interest.

- **Proximity:** Group related elements closer together to establish relationships and improve scannability.
- **Contrast:** Use differences in color, size, and weight to differentiate between important and less important elements.
- **Repetition:** Repeat certain visual elements throughout the interface to create a sense of unity and brand recognition.
- **Alignment:** Align elements to create a sense of order and organization. Even intentional misalignment can be used for emphasis, but with caution.

By applying these principles, you create a visually appealing and intuitive interface that effectively guides user attention.

5.2 Color Theory and User Perception

Colors evoke emotions and influence user perception. Understanding color theory empowers you to use color strategically in your design. Here are some key considerations:

- **Color Psychology:** Different colors have different psychological associations. For example, red is often associated with excitement or urgency, while blue evokes feelings of trust and calmness.

- **Color Contrast:** Ensure adequate contrast between text and background colors for optimal readability, especially for users with visual impairments.

- **Color Schemes:** Develop a limited color palette that complements each other and reinforces your brand identity.

Effective use of color can enhance user experience by making the interface visually appealing and guiding user attention. However, avoid overwhelming users with too many colors or clashing combinations.

5.3 Building a Cohesive Brand Identity

Your brand identity is the visual representation of your brand personality and values. A cohesive brand identity translates seamlessly across all touchpoints, including your website, app, marketing materials, and even social media presence. Here's how visual design contributes to building a strong brand identity:

- **Logo Design:** A well-designed logo is a memorable symbol that represents your brand essence.
- **Typography:** Choosing the right fonts can reflect your brand personality and enhance readability.
- **Imagery:** High-quality and consistent imagery reinforces your brand message and resonates with your target audience.
- **Style Guide:** A style guide documents your brand's visual language, ensuring consistency across all design elements.

By carefully crafting a visual design that aligns with your brand identity, you create a memorable user experience that fosters trust and brand loyalty.

Visual design and branding are powerful tools that go beyond aesthetics. When used strategically, they can enhance usability, build trust, and create a lasting impression on your users. In the next chapter, we'll delve into the world of interaction design, exploring how to create user flows and interactions that are not only functional but also engaging.

CHAPTER 6

INTERACTION DESIGN AND MICROINTERACTIONS

Now that you've established a well-structured and visually appealing interface, it's time to breathe life into it! This chapter explores the realm of interaction design, focusing on user flows, microinteractions, and user feedback mechanisms that create a smooth and engaging user experience.

6.1 Designing User Flows and Task Completion

A user flow maps out the steps a user takes to achieve a specific goal within your product. It's like a roadmap for user interaction, ensuring a logical and efficient journey. Here are some key considerations for user flow design:

- **Identifying User Tasks:** Understand the primary tasks users want to achieve within your interface.
- **Mapping User Journeys:** Create visual representations of the steps users take to complete

each task.

- **Streamlining User Flows:** Identify and eliminate unnecessary steps that could hinder user progress.
- **Consistency:** Maintain consistency in interaction patterns across different user flows.

By designing user flows with a focus on task completion, you ensure your interface empowers users to achieve their goals efficiently and with minimal frustration.

6.2 Microinteractions: The Small Details that Matter

Microinteractions are the subtle, yet impactful, interactions users have with your interface. They can be simple animations, sound cues, or changes in visual elements that provide feedback and guide user actions. While seemingly small, microinteractions play a crucial role in user experience by:

- **Enhancing Usability:** Microinteractions can clarify the outcome of user actions and prevent confusion.
- **Building User Confidence:** Clear microinteractions provide users with a sense of control and understanding.

- **Creating   Engagement:**   Well-designed microinteractions can make interactions feel more enjoyable and dynamic.

Here are some examples of effective microinteractions:

- **Loading animations:** Visually communicate that the system is processing user input.
- **Button feedback:** Change the appearance of a button upon hover or click to confirm user interaction.
- **Progress bars:** Visually indicate the progress of lengthy tasks or downloads.

By crafting thoughtful microinteractions, you elevate the user experience beyond functionality, creating a sense of delight and encouraging further engagement.

6.3 User Feedback and Error Handling

Even the most intuitive interface can encounter user errors. Effective user feedback mechanisms ensure users understand the outcome of their actions and how to navigate potential roadblocks. Here's how to create a user-friendly feedback system:

- **Clear and Concise Messages:** Use clear and easy-to-understand language in error messages.
- **Constructive Guidance:** Offer guidance on how users can correct errors and move forward.
- **Visual Cues:** Use visual elements like icons or color changes to supplement error messages.
- **Preventative Measures:** Where possible, implement design solutions that prevent errors from happening in the first place.

By providing clear user feedback and handling errors gracefully, you minimize frustration and ensure users can continue on their journey within your product.

Interaction design goes beyond just functionality. It's about crafting a conversation between users and your interface. Well-designed user flows, microinteractions, and user feedback mechanisms elevate the user experience, fostering trust and encouraging continued engagement. In the next chapter, we'll explore the importance of designing for inclusivity and accessibility, ensuring your product caters to a diverse range of users.

CHAPTER 7

ACCESSIBILITY AND INCLUSIVITY

In today's diverse world, designing for a single type of user simply isn't enough. This chapter delves into the importance of accessibility and inclusivity, exploring how to create interfaces that cater to a wide range of abilities and needs.

7.1 Designing for Diverse Users and Needs

People interact with technology in various ways and have different abilities. Some users might have visual impairments, hearing difficulties, cognitive differences, or motor limitations. By designing with accessibility and inclusivity in mind, you create a product that is usable by everyone, regardless of their abilities. Here's why it's important:

- **Ethical Responsibility:** Everyone deserves the opportunity to access and use digital products.

- **Wider Audience Reach:** Designing for accessibility expands your potential user base, fostering inclusivity and growth.

- **Enhanced Brand Reputation:** Demonstrating a commitment to accessibility reflects positively on your brand image.

There are various user groups to consider when designing inclusively:

- **Users with Visual Impairments:** Ensure proper color contrast, provide alternative text descriptions for images, and make the interface compatible with screen readers.

- **Users with Hearing Impairments:** Offer closed captions for videos, provide transcripts for audio content, and consider visual cues for important information.

- **Users with Motor Limitations:** Allow for keyboard navigation, avoid overly complex gestures, and ensure touch targets are large enough for easy interaction.

- **Users with Cognitive Differences:** Use clear and concise language, structure content logically, and

· offer alternative ways to complete tasks.

By acknowledging these diverse needs and incorporating accessibility best practices, you create a user experience that is truly inclusive and empowers everyone to participate.

7.2 WCAG Accessibility Guidelines

The Web Content Accessibility Guidelines (WCAG) are a set of internationally recognized standards developed by the World Wide Web Consortium (W3C) to ensure web content is accessible to people with disabilities. These guidelines provide a framework for designing interfaces that are:

- **Perceivable:** Information and user interface components must be presented in a way that can be perceived by users, regardless of their sensory abilities.
- **Operable:** User interface components and navigation must be operable by users, including those using assistive technologies.
- **Understandable:** Information and the operation of

the user interface must be understandable by users.

- **Robust:** Content must remain robust enough to be compatible with a wide range of user agents, including assistive technologies.

While WCAG primarily focuses on web content, the principles can be applied more broadly to the design of digital products across various platforms.

7.3 Making Your Product Usable for Everyone

There's no single solution to guarantee perfect accessibility for everyone. However, by following these principles, you can significantly improve the usability of your product for a wider audience:

- **User Testing with Diverse Participants:** Incorporate users with disabilities into your user testing process to identify and address accessibility issues.
- **Focus on Keyboard Navigation:** Ensure all functionalities can be accessed using just the keyboard for users who rely on assistive technologies.

- **Provide Clear and Concise Language:** Avoid jargon and technical terms, and use clear and simple language that is easy to understand.

- **Offer Alternative Input Methods:** Consider options like voice commands or touchless interactions for users with motor limitations.

- **Regular Testing and Improvement:** Accessibility is an ongoing process. Continuously test your product and iterate based on user feedback.

By embracing inclusivity and actively working towards accessibility, you create a product that is not only usable but also demonstrates your commitment to social responsibility. In the next chapter, we'll explore the ever-evolving world of mobile technology and how to design user interfaces that adapt and optimize for various devices.

CHAPTER 8

DESIGNING FOR MOBILE AND RESPONSIVE INTERFACES

The digital landscape is no longer confined to desktops. Today, users access information and interact with products predominantly through their mobile devices. This chapter explores the principles of responsive design and mobile-first approaches, ensuring your interface seamlessly adapts and delivers an optimal user experience across various screen sizes.

8.1 Responsive Design and Device Optimization

Gone are the days of designing separate interfaces for desktop and mobile. Responsive design has become the standard. It allows your interface to adapt its layout and functionality based on the device being used. Here's how it works:

- **Media Queries:** Media queries are codes that detect the size and type of device accessing the interface.

- **Flexible Layouts:** Elements like grids, images, and text are designed to adjust and resize based on the screen dimensions.

- **Fluid Grid System:** A fluid grid system uses relative units (percentages) to define element sizes and spacing, ensuring proportionate scaling across devices.

- **Breakpoints:** Breakpoints define specific screen sizes where significant layout changes occur to optimize the interface for different device categories (e.g., smartphones, tablets, laptops, desktops).

By implementing responsive design, you ensure a single interface provides a seamless user experience across various devices, eliminating the need for separate mobile apps in some cases.

8.2 Touch-Friendly Interactions and Layouts

Mobile interaction relies primarily on touchscreens. Here's how to design touch-friendly interfaces:

- **Larger Touch Targets:** Ensure buttons, icons, and other interactive elements are large enough for easy and accurate tapping.

- **Proper Spacing:** Maintain adequate space between elements to avoid accidental touches on adjacent elements.

- **Simple and Clear Navigation:** Prioritize primary navigation menus and essential functionalities for easy access on smaller screens.

- **Minimize Scrolling:** Strive for a clear and concise information hierarchy to minimize excessive scrolling on mobile devices.

- **Optimize for Gestures:** Consider common touch gestures like swiping and pinching when designing interactions.

By prioritizing touch-friendliness, you make your interface intuitive and enjoyable to use on mobile devices, catering to the primary mode of user interaction in today's digital world.

8.3 Mobile-First Design Considerations

In a mobile-driven world, some experts advocate for a "mobile-first" design approach. This means prioritizing the design for mobile devices and then scaling it up for larger screens. Here's why it can be beneficial:

- **Focus on Core Functionality:** Designing for mobile first encourages a focus on the most essential functionalities, ensuring a streamlined and efficient user experience.
- **Content Prioritization:** The limited screen space on mobile devices necessitates a clear understanding of what content is most crucial for users.
- **Simplicity Reigns Supreme:** Mobile-first design emphasizes simplicity and clarity, which benefits all users regardless of device.

While responsive design remains the primary approach, a mobile-first mindset can be valuable in ensuring your interface prioritizes core functionalities and delivers an optimal experience on the most widely used devices.

The mobile revolution has transformed how users interact with digital products. By embracing responsive design principles, prioritizing touch-friendliness, and considering a mobile-first approach, you ensure your interface adapts and delivers a seamless user experience across the ever-expanding mobile landscape.

CHAPTER 9

USER TESTING AND ITERATION

The road to exceptional UX/UI design is paved with good intentions and...user testing! No matter how meticulous your planning or polished your design, the true test lies in how real users interact with your interface. This chapter dives deep into the importance of user testing and iteration, the cornerstones of crafting user-centered designs that resonate with your audience.

9.1 The Importance of User Testing

User testing isn't a mere formality; it's a crucial process that unlocks a treasure trove of insights. Here's why you should prioritize user testing:

- **Uncover Hidden Usability Issues:** You, as the designer, might miss potential roadblocks in your interface. User testing reveals these challenges early on, allowing you to address them before launch and prevent user frustration.

- **Validate Design Decisions:** Did you choose the right path for that dropdown menu? User testing helps confirm whether your design choices are intuitive and effective for your target audience.

- **Unlock New Design Opportunities:** Sometimes, the most valuable takeaways from user testing come unexpectedly. Users might reveal unforeseen behaviors or needs that can spark fresh design ideas and ultimately enhance the user experience.

Remember, user testing isn't a one-shot deal. It's an iterative process that should be woven throughout the design journey, from initial prototypes to final stages of development.

9.2 Usability Testing Methods

There's no single "best" method for user testing. The ideal approach depends on your specific needs and resources. Here's a toolbox of popular testing methods:

- **Moderated Usability Testing:** A facilitator

observes users interacting with the interface and guides them through tasks, asking questions to gain insights into their thought processes and challenges encountered.

- **Unmoderated Usability Testing:** This method allows users to complete tasks with the interface remotely, often using screen recording software to capture their interactions and voiceover feedback.

- **A/B Testing:** Present two variations of a design element (e.g., button layout, call-to-action wording) to different user groups and measure which version performs better based on user engagement or task completion rates. This helps you determine the most effective design choice.

- **Card Sorting:** Users categorize information based on their own understanding, revealing how they naturally organize content. This helps you structure your interface in a way that aligns with user expectations.

- **Eye-Tracking:** This technique tracks users' eye movements to understand where their attention focuses on the interface. Eye-tracking can identify areas of confusion or highlight elements that grab user interest.

By employing a combination of these methods, you gain a well-rounded understanding of user behavior and identify areas for improvement.

9.3 Iterating on Your Design Based on User Feedback

Once the user testing dust settles, it's time to analyze the feedback and refine your design. Here's how to approach this critical stage:

- **Identify Common Themes:** Look for patterns and recurring issues raised by users during testing. Are users getting lost in a particular navigation flow? Is a specific form confusing to fill out?
- **Prioritize Changes:** Focus on addressing the most critical usability issues that significantly impact the user experience. Fix the roadblocks that are causing the biggest headaches for your users.
- **Refine Your Design:** Based on user feedback, make changes to the interface. This could involve improving the clarity of instructions, simplifying a complex process, or adjusting the visual hierarchy to

guide user attention more effectively.

- **Retest and Iterate:** Remember, design is a journey, not a destination. After making changes, conduct additional user testing to validate the effectiveness of your iterations. This ensures you're on the right track and continuously improving the user experience.

Embrace the Iterative Cycle

User testing and iteration are the beating heart of UX/UI design. By actively seeking user feedback and using it to refine your designs, you ensure your interface evolves and adapts to meet the needs of your users. This ongoing process is the key to creating user experiences that are not only functional but also enjoyable and engaging.

CHAPTER 10

The Future of UX/UI Design

The world of UX/UI design is constantly evolving, driven by technological advancements and ever-changing user expectations. This chapter explores some of the exciting trends shaping the future of UX/UI design, highlighting the growing importance of user experience (UX) writing and the potential impact of artificial intelligence (AI).

10.1 Emerging Trends in UX/UI Design

The future of UX/UI design is brimming with possibilities. Here are some key trends to watch:

- **Voice User Interfaces (VUIs):** Voice assistants like Siri and Alexa are becoming increasingly popular. Designing interfaces that respond to natural voice commands will be crucial for a seamless user experience.

- **Conversational Interfaces (CIs):** CIs take VUIs a

step further, allowing users to engage in natural conversations with chatbots or virtual assistants to complete tasks or access information.

- **Microinteractions and User Delight:** The focus on crafting subtle yet impactful microinteractions that enhance user engagement and evoke positive emotions will continue to grow.

- **Personalization and User-Centered Design:** Tailoring the user experience to individual needs and preferences will be paramount. This may involve using data to personalize content, interfaces, and interactions.

- **Augmented Reality (AR) and Virtual Reality (VR):** As AR and VR technologies mature, they will play a more significant role in UX/UI design, creating immersive user experiences that blur the lines between the physical and digital worlds.

These trends emphasize the importance of designing for a future where users interact with technology in ever-more nuanced and dynamic ways.

10.2 The Rise of User Experience (UX) Writing

The power of words cannot be underestimated in UX/UI design. UX writing goes beyond simple labels and instructions. It's about crafting clear, concise, and engaging language that guides users through the interface, informs decisions, and ultimately enhances the user experience. Here's why UX writing is becoming increasingly important:

- **Clarity and Usability:** Well-written text ensures users understand the interface, can complete tasks efficiently, and avoid confusion.
- **Emotional Connection:** The right words can build trust, establish brand voice, and create a positive emotional connection with users.
- **Accessibility:** Clear and concise language is crucial for users with disabilities or those with limited language proficiency.
- **Search Engine Optimization (SEO):** UX writing that incorporates relevant keywords can improve the discoverability of your product or service in search engines.

Investing in skilled UX writers ensures the user experience is not just functional but also clear, engaging, and resonates with your target audience.

10.3 The Impact of Artificial Intelligence (AI) on UX/UI Design

Artificial intelligence is poised to significantly impact UX/UI design in the following ways:

- **Personalization:** AI can analyze user data to personalize the user experience, recommending content, suggesting features, and tailoring interfaces based on individual preferences.

- **Accessibility Improvements:** AI-powered tools can assist with tasks like image recognition and text-to-speech conversion, improving accessibility for users with disabilities.

- **User Interface Optimization:** AI algorithms can analyze user behavior and identify areas for improvement in the interface, leading to a more efficient and user-friendly experience.

- **Content Creation and Chatbots:** AI can be used to generate content that adapts to user needs and develop chatbots that can engage with users in a more natural and personalized way.

However, it's important to remember that AI is a tool, not a replacement for human creativity and empathy. The future of UX/UI design lies in a harmonious collaboration between human designers and AI, leveraging technology's power to enhance, not replace, human creativity.

Conclusion

The future of UX/UI design is exciting and full of potential. By staying informed about emerging trends, embracing the power of UX writing, and utilizing AI as a valuable tool, you can create user experiences that are not only functional but also innovative, engaging, and leave a lasting positive impression on your users. This concludes our exploration of UX/UI design. Remember, the journey of design is a continuous learning process. Keep exploring, keep experimenting, and keep pushing the boundaries to create user experiences that shape a better future.

ABOUT THE AUTHOR

Writer's Bio:

 Benjamin Evans, a respected figure in the tech world, is known for his insightful commentary and analysis. With a strong educational background likely in fields such as computer science, engineering, or business, he brings a depth of knowledge to his discussions on emerging technologies and industry trends. Evans' knack for simplifying complex concepts, coupled with his innate curiosity and passion for innovation, has established him as a go-to source for understanding the dynamics of the digital landscape. Through articles, speeches, and social media, he shares his expertise and offers valuable insights into the impact of technology on society.

www.ingramcontent.com/pod-product-compliance
Lightning Source LLC
LaVergne TN
LVHW051619050326
832903LV00033B/4579